Topsy + Tim

Learn to count

Jean and Gareth Adamson

1

one

One dear old donkey with Topsy and Tim.

Both in the saddle, so let's begin.

Published by Ladybird Books Ltd
27 Wrights Lane London W8 5TZ
A Penguin Company

2 4 6 8 10 9 7 5 3 1

First published MCMLXXXII © Jean and Gareth Adamson
This edition MMI

Printed in Italy

Two pumpkin lanterns can give you a fright,
But these are smiling, so that's all right.

3
three

Three tiny seedlings – what will they be?

A poppy, a sunflower – and maybe a TREE!

4

four

Four fish swim in a little pool.

Water weeds keep them happy and cool.

5
five

Way up high, in the sky,
Five butterflies flutter by.

6

six

Six fat sausages sizzling in a pan,

Three went 'pop' and the rest went 'BANG!'

7

seven

Seven stairs. It's bedtime already.

Goodnight Kitty, from the twins and Teddy.

8
eight

Eight candles on this birthday cake.

Twins have a double wish to make.

9
nine

Nine jam tarts, all ready to eat.

Tim licks the spoon for an extra treat.

10

ten

Ten tiny tadpoles wriggling about.

They'll turn into frogs and then – watch out!

11
eleven

Eleven lights on the Christmas tree.

Is Santa coming? Wait and see!

12

twelve

We're buttoned up for wintry weather.

Look – twelve buttons altogether.

13
thirteen

Thirteen bees fly home past our tree.

Will they have honey for their tea?

14

fourteen

Fourteen shells on the sandy shore.

Tim says he can find lots more.

15

fifteen

Topsy and Tim have lost fifteen sheep,
Like little Boy Blue and little Bo Peep.

16

sixteen

Sixteen squares make a quilt so bright,
To keep us warm all through the night.

17

seventeen

Seventeen sparrows, hungry as can be.

Here are the breadcrumbs for your tea.

18

eighteen

Eighteen apples on the tree so tall.

Hold on Topsy or you'll fall.

19
nineteen

Nineteen stars in the night sky gleaming.

Topsy and Tim are quietly dreaming.

20
twenty

Twenty toes. How many have you?

If you were twins, you'd have twenty toes too.

Use your finger to follow the stepping stones through Topsy and Tim's garden.

Say each number out loud as you go.

Can you count how many babies each
animal has?

Tim's drawn a picture. Can you find these things in it?

1 sandcastle 2 starfish 3 boats
4 shells 5 seagulls

Count the apples on the tree.
How many are red?
How many are green?
How many altogether?

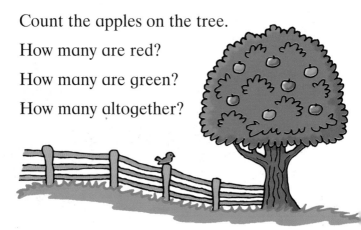

Little Bo Peep has found five of her sheep.

There are five more still missing.

Can you find them in the big picture?

1	2	3
one	two	three

6	7
six	seven

11	12	13
eleven	twelve	thirteen

16	17
sixteen	seventeen